D1042692

EXPRESSIONS
OF
Hope

EXPRESSIONS
OF
Hope

Helen Steiner Rice

BARBOUR
PUBLISHING

© 2007 by the Helen Steiner Rice Foundation

ISBN 978-1-59789-827-0

Devotional writing by Rebecca Currington in association with Snapdragon Group℠ Editorial Services.

The poetry of Helen Steiner Rice is published under a licensing agreement with the Helen Steiner Rice Foundation.

Special thanks to Virginia Ruehlmann for her cooperation and assistance in the development of this book.

Published by Barbour Publishing, Inc., P.O. Box 719, Uhrichsville, Ohio 44683 www.barbourbooks.com

Our mission is to publish and distribute inspirational products offering exceptional value and biblical encouragement to the masses.

 Member of the Evangelical Christian Publishers Association

Printed in Malaysia.

Contents

Prayer

"If you believe, you will receive whatever you ask for in prayer."

MATTHEW 21:22

It must break God's heart when He sees so many people praying to gods of stone—gods who cannot hear their pleas or help them find their way. Your God is a living God. He listens to your prayers with a heart of love. When you kneel before Him, you can feel the comforting warmth of His presence. It is then that you know you have placed your hope in the One True God—the God who hears and helps.

Just close your eyes and open your heart

And feel your worries and cares depart,

Just yield yourself to the Father above

And let Him hold you secure in His love.

So when you are tired, discouraged, and blue,

There's always one door that is open to you—

For the heart is a temple when God is there

As we place ourselves in His loving care.

$\mathcal{K}$neel in prayer in His presence,

and you'll find no need to speak,

For softly in quiet communion,

God grants you the peace that you seek.

For when we seek shelter in
    His wondrous love,
And we ask Him to send us
    help from above. . .
And that is the reason
    we know it is true
That bright, shining hours and
    dark, sad ones, too,
Are part of the plan
    God made for each one,
And all we can pray is,
    "Thy will be done."
And know that you are never alone,
For God is your Father and
    you're one of His own.

Brighten your day

And lighten your way

And lessen your cares

With daily prayers.

Quiet your mind

And leave tension behind

And find inspiration

In hushed meditation.

Whenever we're troubled and lost in despair,

We have but to seek Him and ask Him in prayer

To guide and direct us and help us to bear

Our sickness and sorrow, our worry and care.

Prayers are the stairs that lead to God,

and there's joy every step of the way

When we make our pilgrimage to Him

with love in our hearts each day.

Although it sometimes seems to us

our prayers have not been heard,

God always knows our every need

without a single word,

And He will not forsake us,

a tender watch to keep. . .

And in good time He'll answer us,

and in His love He'll send

Greater things than we have asked

and blessings without end.

Whenever I am troubled

and lost in deep despair,

I bundle all my troubles up

and go to God in prayer. . .

I know He stilled the tempest

and calmed the angry sea,

And I humbly ask if, in His love,

He'll do the same for me. . .

And then I just keep quiet

and think only thoughts of peace,

And as I abide in stillness

my restless murmurings cease.

Prayer is so often just words unspoken,
Whispered in tears
    by a heart that is broken,
For God is already deeply aware
Of the burdens we find
    too heavy to bear. . .
And all we need do
    is seek Him in prayer
And without a word
    He will help us to bear
Our trials and troubles,
    our sickness and sorrow
And show us the way
    to a brighter tomorrow.
There's no need at all
    for impressive prayer,
For the minute we seek God
    He's already there.

THERE IS ONLY ONE PLACE

AND ONLY ONE FRIEND

WHO IS NEVER TOO BUSY,

AND YOU CAN ALWAYS DEPEND

ON HIM TO BE WAITING,

WITH ARMS OPEN WIDE,

TO HEAR ALL THE TROUBLES

YOU CAME TO CONFIDE.

FOR THE HEAVENLY FATHER

WILL ALWAYS BE THERE

WHEN YOU SEEK HIM AND FIND HIM

AT THE ALTAR OF PRAYER.

Do not be anxious about anything,
but in everything, by prayer and
petition, with thanksgiving,
present your requests to God.

PHILPPIANS 4:6

Though we feel helpless

    and alone when we start,

A prayer is the key that opens the heart,

And as the heart opens,

    the dear Lord comes in

And the prayer that we felt

    we could never begin

It is so easy to say,

    for the Lord understands

And He gives us new strength

    by the touch of His hands.

On the wings of prayer

our burdens take flight,

And our load of care

becomes bearably light,

And our heavy hearts are lifted above

To be healed by the balm

of God's wonderful love.

There's no problem too big

    and no question too small—

Just ask God in faith

    and He'll answer them all—

Not always at once,

    so be patient and wait,

For God never comes

    too soon or too late. . .

So trust in His wisdom

    and believe in His Word,

For no prayer's unanswered

    and no prayer's unheard.

I cannot dwell apart from You—

You would not ask or want me to,

For You have room within Your heart

To make each child of Yours a part

Of You and all Your love and care

If we but come to You in prayer.

23

Eternal Life

Your heavenly Father has given you life, dear friend—and not just life, but *eternal* life. Your body will die and be replaced by one far better. For those who place their hope in Him, death holds no threat. . . no sting. It is simply a transition from one form of life to another. He shepherds us as we pass through the Valley of the Shadow of Death, proving that death really is just a shadow—one that vanishes in the light of His presence.

Nothing really ever dies
      that is not born anew
The miracles of nature
      all tell us this is true. . .
The flowers sleeping peacefully
      beneath the winter's snow
Awaken from their icy grave
      when spring winds start to blow
And all around on every side
      new life and joy appear
To tell us nothing ever dies
      and we should have no fear,
For death is just a detour
      along life's wending way
That leads God's chosen children
      to a bright and glorious day.

Death is only a stepping-stone

To a beautiful life

   we have never known—

A place where God

   promised man he would be

Eternally happy and safe and free.

To know that life is endless

puts new purpose in our days

And fills our hearts with joyous songs

of hope and love and praise.

We all have many things to be

deeply thankful for,

But God's everlasting promise

of life forevermore

Is a reason for thanksgiving

every hour of the day

As we walk toward eternal life

along the King's highway.

*Give thanks to the L*ORD*, for he is good.*
His love endures forever.

PSALM 136:1

We cannot see the future,

what's beyond is still unknown,

For the secret of God's kingdom

still belongs to Him alone.

But He granted us salvation

when His Son was crucified,

For life became immortal

because our Savior died.

Death is a time of sleeping,

For those who die are in God's keeping,

And there's a sunrise for each soul—

For life, not death,

   is God's promised goal. . .

So trust God's promise

   and doubt Him never,

For only through death

   can man live forever.

I am the Way, so just follow Me

Though the way be rough

   and you cannot see. . .

I am the Truth which all men seek,

So heed not false prophets nor the

   words that they speak. . .

I am the Life, and I hold the key

That opens the door to eternity. . .

And in this dark world, I am the Light

To the Promised Land

   where there is no night.

He carried the cross to Calvary—

Carried its burden for you and me.

There on the cross He was crucified,

And because He bled and died,

We know that whatever our cross may be,

It leads to God and eternity.

In that fair city that God has prepared

Are unending joys to be happily shared

With all of our loved ones

who patiently wait

On death's other side to open the gate.

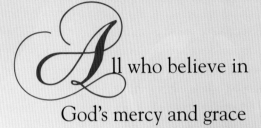

All who believe in

God's mercy and grace

Will meet their loved ones face-to-face

Where time is endless and joy unbroken

And only the words of

God's love are spoken.

He who safely brought me here
Will also take me safely back.
And though in many things I lack,
He will not let me go alone
Into the valley that's unknown. . .
So I reach out and take Death's hand
And journey to the Promised Land.

Man and woman, like flowers, too,

    must sleep

Until called from the darkened deep

To live in that place where angels sing

And where there is eternal spring.

There is no night without a dawning,
    no winter without a spring
And beyond death's dark horizon,
    our hearts will once more sing.
For those who leave us for a while
    have only gone away
Out of a restless, careworn world
    into a brighter day
Where there will be no partings
    and time is not counted by years,
Where there are no trials or troubles,
    no worries, no cares, and no tears.

Man is but born to die and arise
For beyond this world in beauty there lies
The purpose of death, which is but to gain
Life everlasting in God's great domain. . .
And no one need make this journey alone,
For God has promised to take care of His own.
Live for Me and die for Me,
And I, your God, will set you free!

God's Faithfulness

Your word, O LORD, is eternal; it stands firm in the heavens. Your faithfulness continues through all generations; you established the earth, and it endures.

PSALM 119:89–90

People—even those you love the most—will fail you. And you will fail them. That's how it is with human beings. But God is another story. If you put your hope in Him one hundred times, you will find Him faithful one hundred times. The more you hope in His goodness, the more you find Him utterly faithful without exception. What a wonderful thing it is to know you are trusting in the One who will never—can never—let you down.

Then in Thy goodness and mercy,

    look down on this weak, erring one

And tell me that I am forgiven

    for all I've so willfully done,

And teach me to humbly start following

    the path that the dear Savior trod

So I'll find at the end of life's journey

    a home in the city of God.

After the clouds, the sunshine,

After the winter, the spring,

After the shower, the rainbow—

For life is a changeable thing;

After the night, the morning

Bidding all darkness cease

After life's cares and sorrow,

The comfort and sweetness of peace.

Whatever our problems,

troubles, and sorrows,

If we trust in the Lord,

there'll be brighter tomorrows

For there's nothing too much

for the great God to do,

And all that He asks or expects from you

Is faith that's unshaken

by tribulations and tears

That keeps growing stronger

along with the years.

$\mathcal{T}$rust in His wisdom

and believe in His word,

For no prayer's unanswered

and no prayer unheard.

Now faith is being sure of what we hope for and certain of what we do not see. . . . And without faith it is impossible to please God, because anyone who comes to him must believe that he exists and that he rewards those who earnestly seek him.

HEBREWS 11:1, 6

Wait with a heart that is patient

for the goodness of God to prevail—

For never do prayers go unanswered,

and His mercy and love never fail.

Cast your cares on the Lord and he will sustain you; he will never let the righteous fall.

We often feel deserted

    in times of deep stress

Without God's presence

    to assure us and bless,

And it is when our senses are reeling

We realize clearly

    it's faith and not feeling,

For it takes great faith

    to patiently wait,

Believing God comes

    not too soon or too late.

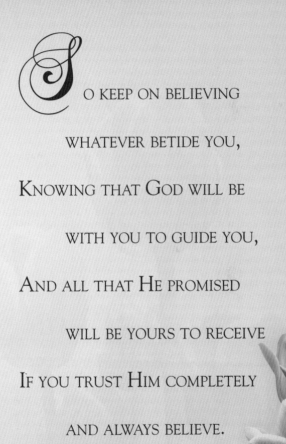

$\mathcal{S}$O KEEP ON BELIEVING

WHATEVER BETIDE YOU,

KNOWING THAT GOD WILL BE

WITH YOU TO GUIDE YOU,

AND ALL THAT HE PROMISED

WILL BE YOURS TO RECEIVE

IF YOU TRUST HIM COMPLETELY

AND ALWAYS BELIEVE.

53

The rainbow is God's promise

of hope for you and me,

And though the clouds hang heavy

and the sun we cannot see,

We know above the dark clouds

that fill the stormy sky

Hope's rainbow will come shining through

when the clouds have drifted by.

And so today I walk with God

Because I love Him so. . .

If I have faith and trust in Him

There's nothing I need to know.

The Lord is our salvation

And our strength in every fight,

Our redeemer and protector,

Our eternal guiding light. . .

He has promised to sustain us,

He's our refuge from all harms,

And underneath this refuge

Are the everlasting arms.

"Do not store up for yourselves treasures on earth, where moth and rust destroy, and where thieves break in and steal. But store up for yourselves treasures in heaven, where moth and rust do not destroy, and where thieves do not break in and steal. For where your treasure is, there your heart will be also."

MATTHEW 6:19–21

The silent stars in timeless skies,

The wonderment in children's eyes,

The autumn haze, the breath of spring,

The chirping song the crickets sing,

A rosebud in a slender vase

Are all reflections of God's face.

$\mathcal{K}$ nowing God's love is unfailing,

and His mercy unending and great,

You have but to trust in His promise—

God comes not too soon or too late.

For when we are helpless

    with no place to go

And our hearts are heavy

    and our spirits are low,

If we place our lives in God's hands

And surrender completely

    to His will and demands,

The darkness lifts

    and the sun shines through,

And by His touch we are born anew.

There's truly nothing we need know

If we have faith wherever we go,

God will be there to help us bear

Our disappointments, pain, and care,

For He is our shepherd,

    our Father, our guide—

You're never alone with

    the Lord at your side.

God's Love

*"I have loved you with an everlasting love;
I have drawn you with loving-kindness."*

JEREMIAH 31:3

Human love is a wonderful thing—
exciting, inspiring, intense—but often
fickle. God's love, on the other hand,
is constant. It never changes. . .solid
bedrock from beginning to end. God
loves you simply because you are His. He
created you, and when you went astray,
He bought you back at a great price. His
love is based on His mercy rather than
your merit. A love that will remain strong
today, tomorrow, and for eternity.

We are all God's children

and He loves us, every one.

He freely and completely forgives

all that we have done,

Asking only if we're ready

to follow where He leads,

Content that in His wisdom

He will answer all our needs.

What is love? No words can define it—
It's something so great
    only God could design it.
For love means much more
    than small words can express,
For what we call love is very much less
Than the beauty and depth
    and the true richness of
God's gift to mankind—
    His compassionate love.

Somebody loves you more than you know,

Somebody goes with you wherever you go,

Somebody really and truly cares

And lovingly listens to all of your prayers.

And if you walk in His footsteps

and have faith to believe,

There's nothing you ask for

that you will not receive.

Kings and kingdoms all pass away—

Nothing on earth endures. . .

But the love of God who sent His Son

Is forever and ever yours!

His love knows no exceptions,

so never feel excluded—

No matter who or what you are,

your name has been included.

The sky and the stars,
   the waves and the sea,
The dew on the grass,
   the leaves on the tree
Are constant reminders
   of God and His nearness,
Proclaiming His presence
   with crystal-like clearness.
So how could I think God
   was far, far away
When I feel Him beside me
   every hour of the day?
And I've plenty of reasons
   to know God's my friend,
And this is one friendship
   that time cannot end!

God's love is like an island in

life's ocean vast and wide—

A peaceful, quiet shelter from

the restless, rising tide.

God's love is like a fortress,

and we seek protection there

When the waves of tribulation

seem to drown us in despair.

71

God's love is like a sanctuary where our

souls can find sweet rest

From the struggle and the tension of

life's fast and futile quest.

God's love is like a beacon burning

bright with faith and prayer,

And through the changing scenes of life

we can find a haven there.

Be imitators of God, therefore, as dearly loved children and live a life of love.

EPHESIANS 5:1–2

No matter what your past has been,
Trust God to understand.
And no matter what your problem is
Just place it in His hand—
For in all of our unloveliness
This great God loves us still.
He loved us since the world began
And what's more, He always will.

WHAT MORE CAN WE ASK OF OUR FATHER

THAN TO KNOW WE ARE NEVER ALONE,

THAT HIS MERCY AND LOVE ARE UNFAILING,

AND HE MAKES ALL OUR PROBLEMS HIS OWN.

Friendship and Love

Whoever loves his brother lives in the light, and there is nothing in him to make him stumble.

1 JOHN 2:10

The miracle of God's love for us is more than we could ever have asked or imagined, and yet He has given above and beyond. He has given us friends to warm our hearts and stand beside us in the good times and the bad, to bring us hope and encouragement. God revels in the love we have for each other and encourages, even commands, us to love each other as He has loved us. What a generous God we serve.

77

Among the great and glorious gifts

    our heavenly Father sends

Is the gift of understanding that

    we find in loving friends,

For it's not money or gifts

    or material things,

But understanding the joy it brings,

That can change this old world

    in wonderful ways

And put goodness and mercy

    back in our days.

Friendship is a priceless gift

That can't be bought or sold,

But to have an understanding friend

Is worth far more than gold.

Thank you for your friendship

And your understanding of

The folks who truly love you

And the folks you truly love.

Friends and prayers are priceless treasures

Beyond all monetary measures,

And so I say a special prayer

That God will keep you in His care.

Like ships upon the sea of life

 we meet with friends so dear,

Then sail on swiftly from the ones

 we'd like to linger near;

Sometimes I wish the winds would cease,

 the waves be quiet, too,

And let me sort of drift along

 beside a friend like you.

Just like a sunbeam brightens the sky,

A smile on the face of a passerby

Can make a drab and crowded street

A pleasant place where two smiles meet.

Rejoice in the Lord always.
I will say it again: Rejoice!

PHILIPPIANS 4:4

THE MORE OF EVERYTHING YOU SHARE,

THE MORE YOU'LL ALWAYS HAVE TO SPARE. . .

FOR ONLY WHAT YOU GIVE AWAY

ENRICHES YOU FROM DAY TO DAY!

There are things we cannot measure,

Like the depths of waves and sea

And the heights of stars in heaven

And the joy you bring to me. . .

Like eternity's long endlessness

And the sunset's golden hue,

There is no way to measure

The love I have for you.

An unlit candle gives no light,

Only when it's burning

   is it shining bright.

And life is empty, dull, and dark,

Until doing things for others

   gives the needed spark

That sets a useless life on fire

And fills the heart with new desire.

Friendship, like flowers,

blooms ever more fair

When carefully tended by

dear friends who care;

And life's lovely garden

would be sweeter by far

If all who passed through it

were as nice as you are.

For every day's a good day

    to lose yourself in others

And any time a good time

    to see mankind as brothers,

And this can only happen when

    you realize it's true

That everyone needs someone

    and that someone is you.

Across the years we've met in dreams

And shared each other's hopes and schemes,

We knew a friendship rich and rare

And beauty far beyond compare.

Then you reached out your arms for more,

To catch what you were yearning for.

But little did you think or guess

That one can't capture happiness

Because it's unrestrained and free,

Unfettered by reality.

We lock up our hearts and fail to heed
The outstretched hand, reaching to find
A kindred spirit whose heart and mind
Are lonely and longing
    to somehow share
Our joys and sorrows
    and to make us aware
That life's completeness
    and richness depends
On the things we share with
    our loved ones and friends.

Gold is cold and lifeless,
        it cannot see nor hear,
And in your times of trouble,
        it is powerless to cheer.
It has no ears to listen,
        no heart to understand.
It cannot bring you comfort
        or reach out a helping hand.
So when you ask God for a gift,
        be thankful that He sends,
Not diamonds, pearls, or riches,
        but the love of a real, true friend.

If people like me didn't
know people like you,
Life would lose its meaning
and its richness, too.
For the friends that we make
are life's gifts of love,
And I think friends are sent
right from heaven above.
And thinking of you
somehow makes me feel
That God is love and He's very real.

For in this world of trouble

    that is filled with anxious care,

Everybody needs a friend

    in whom they're free to share,

The little secret heartaches

    that lay heavy on their mind,

We seek our true and trusted friend

    in the knowledge that we'll find

A heart that's sympathetic

    and an understanding mind.

Like roses in a garden,
    kindness fills the air
With a certain bit of sweetness
    as it touches everywhere.
For kindness is a circle that never,
    never ends
But just keeps ever-widening
    in the circle of our friends.
For the more you give, the more you get
    is proven every day,
And so to get the most from life
    you must give yourself away.

You're like a ray of sunshine

Or a star up in the sky,

You add a special brightness

Whenever you pass by.

For in this raucous, restless world

We're small but God is great,

And in His love, dear friend,

Our hearts communicate!

Father, make us kind and wise

So we may always recognize

The blessings that are ours to take,

The friendships that are ours to make,

If we but open our heart's door wide

To let the sunshine of love inside.

Nothing on earth can make

life more worthwhile

Than a true, loyal friend

and the warmth of a smile,

For, just like a sunbeam makes

the cloudy days brighter,

The smile of a friend makes

a heavy heart lighter.

Courage

"This is my command—be strong and courageous! Do not be afraid or discouraged. For the LORD your God is with you wherever you go."

JOSHUA 1:9 NLT

Does your heart feel faint with fear when faced with the challenges of this life? The truth is, we all have fainting hearts—even the biggest, bravest people among us. But we need not fear anything when God is on our side. Our courage is not vested in our limited capabilities but in His mighty power. Our heavenly Father fights for us. Place your faith and your hope in Him.

BLESSED ARE THE PEOPLE

   WHO LEARN TO ACCEPT

THE TROUBLE MEN TRY

   TO ESCAPE AND REJECT,

FOR IN OUR ACCEPTANCE

   WE'RE GIVEN GREAT GRACE

AND COURAGE AND FAITH

   AND THE STRENGTH TO FACE

THE DAILY TROUBLES THAT COME TO US ALL,

SO WE MAY LEARN TO

   STAND STRAIGHT AND TALL.

$\mathcal{W}$rapped within His kindness

you are sheltered and secure

And under His direction

your way is safe and sure.

They tell me that prayer helps
to quiet the mind
And to unburden the heart,
for in stillness we find
A newborn assurance that
Someone does care
And Someone does answer
each small, sincere prayer!

In this age of unrest,

    with danger all around,

We need Thy hand to lead us

    to higher, safer ground. . .

We need Thy help and counsel

    to make us more aware

That our safety and security

    lie solely in Thy care.

Give us strength and courage

to be honorable and true

Practicing Your precepts

in everything we do.

And keep us gently humble in

the greatness of Thy love

So someday we are fit to dwell

with Thee in peace above.

When seen through God's eyes,

earthly troubles diminish,

And we're given new strength

to face and to finish

Life's daily tasks as they come along,

If we but pray for strength

to keep us strong.

Let us then approach the throne of grace with confidence, so that we may receive mercy and find grace to help us in our time of need.

HEBREWS 4:16

You are ushering in another day

untouched and freshly new

So here I come to ask You, God,

if You'll renew me, too.

And Father, I am well aware

I can't make it on my own,

So take my hand and hold it tight,

for I can't walk alone.

Always remember, the hills ahead

   are never as steep as they seem,

And with faith in your heart start

   upward and climb till you reach

   your dream.

Though the way ahead seems steep

Be not afraid, for He will keep

Tender watch through night and day

And He will hear each prayer you pray.

CAST YOUR BURDEN ON HIM,

SEEK HIS COUNSEL WHEN DISTRESSED,

AND GO TO HIM FOR COMFORT

WHEN YOU'RE LONELY AND OPPRESSED—

FOR GOD IS OUR ENCOURAGEMENT

IN TROUBLES AND IN TRIALS,

AND IN SUFFERING AND IN SORROW

HE WILL TURN OUR TEARS TO SMILES.

Growing trees are strengthened when
　　they withstand the storm,
And the sharp cut of a chisel gives the
　　marble grace and form.
God never hurts us needlessly and He
　　never wastes our pain,
For every loss He sends to us is
　　followed by rich gain.
So whenever we are troubled and when
　　everything goes wrong,
It is just God working in us to
　　make our spirits strong.

Nothing is ever too hard to do

If your faith is strong and

your purpose is true. . .

So never give up and never stop,

Just journey on to the mountaintop.

*G*od, grant me. . .

Courage and hope for every day,

Faith to guide me along my way

Understanding and wisdom, too,

And grace to accept what life

gives me to do.

Faith

Jesus said to the disciples, "Have faith in God. I tell you the truth, you can say to this mountain, 'May you be lifted up and thrown into the sea,' and it will happen."

MARK 11:22–23 NLT

While faith and hope are twin virtues—both affect how we receive from God—they have at least one big difference. While hope is quiet, patient, and accustomed to waiting, faith speaks out, takes action, and moves mountains. Both are God's gifts to equip us for successful lives here on earth. Hope in God, dear friend, then invest your faith in His precious promises. It's a winning combination.

Faith to believe when the way is rough

And faith to hang on when

    the going is tough

Will never fail to pull us through

And bring us strength and comfort, too.

Faith makes it wholly possible

to quietly endure

The violent world around us

for in God we are secure.

THOUGH I CANNOT FIND YOUR HAND

TO LEAD ME ON TO THE PROMISED LAND,

I STILL BELIEVE WITH ALL MY BEING

YOUR HAND IS THERE BEYOND MY SEEING.

All who have God's blessing

can rest safely in His care,

For He promises safe passage on

the wings of faith and prayer.

*Let us fix our eyes on Jesus,
the author and perfecter of our faith.*

HEBREWS 12:2

Faith is a force that is greater

Than knowledge or power or skill. . .

And the darkest defeat turns to triumph

If we trust in God's wisdom and will.

Take heart and meet each minute

with faith in God's great love,

Aware that every day of life

is controlled by God above...

And never dread tomorrow

or what the future brings—

Just pray for strength and courage

and trust God in all things.

When the darkness shuts out the light,

We must lean on faith

to restore our sight,

For there is nothing we need to know

If we have faith that wherever we go

God will be there to help us bear

Our disappointments, pain, and care.

Faith in things we cannot see

Requires a child's simplicity.

For faith alone can save man's soul

And lead him to a higher goal,

For there's but one unfailing source—

We win by faith and not by force.

No day is too dark and no burden too great
That God in His love cannot penetrate. . .
And to know and believe
    without question or doubt
That no matter what happens
    God is there to help out
Is to hold in your hand the golden key
To peace and joy and serenity.

For with patience to wait
and faith to endure,
Your life will be blessed
and your future secure,
For God is but testing
your faith and your love
Before He appoints you to rise far above
All the small things
that so sorely distress you,
For God's only intention is
to strengthen and bless you.

It's easy to grow downhearted when

nothing goes your way.

It's easy to be discouraged

when you have a troublesome day.

But trouble is only a challenge

to spur you on to achieve

The best that God has to offer

if you have the faith to believe.

Sometimes when faith is running low

And I cannot fathom why things are so. . .

I walk alone among the flowers I grow

And learn the answers

    to all I would know. . .

For among my flowers I have come to see

Life's miracle and its mystery. . .

And standing in silence and reverie

My faith comes flooding back to me.

WITH FAITH, LET GO AND LET GOD LEAD THE WAY

INTO A BRIGHTER AND LESS-TROUBLED DAY.

FOR GOD HAS A PLAN FOR EVERYONE,

IF WE LEARN TO PRAY, "THY WILL BE DONE."

When our hearts are heavy
    with worry and care
And we are lost in
    the depths of despair. . .
That is the time when faith alone
Can lead us out of the dark unknown.
For faith to believe
    when the way is rough
And faith to hang on
    when the going is tough
Will never fail to pull us through
And bring us strength and comfort, too.

*A*ll we really ever need

Is faith as a grain of mustard seed,

For all God asks is do you believe—

For if you do, you shall receive.

No one discovers the fullness or
    the greatness of God's love
Unless they have walked in the darkness
    with only a light from above.
For the faith to endure whatever comes
    is born of sorrow and trials
And strengthened only by discipline
    and nurtured by self-denials.
So be not disheartened by troubles,
    for trials are the building blocks
On which to erect a fortress of faith
    secure on God's ageless rocks.

Faith is a force that is greater

Than knowledge or power or skill,

And many defeats turn to triumphs

If you trust in God's wisdom and will.

For faith is a mover of mountains—

There's nothing that God cannot do—

So start out today

    with faith in your heart,

And climb till your dreams come true.

We are hard pressed on every side,
but not crushed; perplexed, but not in
despair; persecuted, but not abandoned;
struck down, but not destroyed.

2 CORINTHIANS 4:8–9

Renewal

My health may fail, and my spirit may grow weak, but God remains the strength of my heart; he is mine forever.

PSALM 73:26 NLT

Like a charger hooked up to a battery, the Holy Spirit dwells within us, renewing us day by day. Renewal is not something to save for a retreat; God designed it to be a constant, keeping us always in tune with Him and His purpose for our lives. When the world around you is especially harsh, when your heart is ready to break and you wonder if all is lost, look inside. Ask the Holy Spirit to restore your hope.

Thank You, God, for the beauty

around me everywhere,

The gentle rain and glistening dew,

the sunshine and the air,

The joyous gift of feeling the

soul's soft, whispering voice

That speaks to me from deep within

and makes my heart rejoice.

THERE IS NO NIGHT WITHOUT DAWNING,

NO WINTER WITHOUT A SPRING,

AND BEYOND DEATH'S DARK HORIZON

OUR HEARTS ONCE MORE WILL SING.

Cast your burden on Him,

    seek His counsel when distressed,

And go to Him for comfort

    when you're lonely and oppressed.

For God is our encouragement

    in troubles and in trials,

And in suffering and in sorrow

    He will turn our tears to smiles.

Hope for a world grown cynically cold,

Hungry for power

and greedy for gold—

Faith to believe when,

within and without,

There's a nameless fear

in a world of doubt—

Love that is bigger than race or creed

To cover the world and fulfill each need.

𝒴ou are so great. . .

We are so small. . .

And when trouble comes as it

does to us all

There's so little that we can do

Except to place

our trust in You.

Open your heart's door

and let Christ come in,

And He'll give you new life

and free you from sin—

And there is no joy

that can ever compare

With the joy of knowing

you're in God's care.

For it is by grace you have been saved, through faith—and this not from yourselves, it is the gift of God—not by works, so that no one can boast.

EPHESIANS 2:8–9

147

Why am I cast down and despondently sad
When I long to be happy
    and joyous and glad?
Why is my heart heavy
    with unfathomable weight
As I try to escape this soul-saddened state?
And then, with God's help
    it all becomes clear,
The soul has its seasons
    just the same as the year.
But meeting these seasons of dark desolation
With strength that is born of anticipation
That comes from knowing that
    autumn-time sadness
Will surely be followed by
a springtime of gladness.

148

Each day at dawning I lift my heart high
And raise my eyes to the infinite sky,
I watch the night vanish as a new day is born,
And I hear the birds sing
    on the wings of the morn.
I see the dew glisten in crystal-like splendor
While God, with a touch
    that is gentle and tender,
Wraps up the night and softly tucks it away
And hangs out the sun to herald a new day. . .
And so I give thanks and
    my heart kneels to pray,
"God, keep me and guide me
    and go with me today."

YOU WALK WITH ME AND TALK WITH ME,

FOR I AM YOURS ETERNALLY,

AND WHEN I STUMBLE, SLIP, AND FALL

BECAUSE I'M WEAK AND LOST AND SMALL,

YOU HELP ME UP AND TAKE MY HAND

AND LEAD ME TOWARD THE PROMISED LAND.

In prayer there is renewal of

the spirit, mind, and heart

For everything is lifted up

in which God has a part. . .

For when we go to God in prayer

our thoughts are rearranged,

So even though our problems have not

been solved or changed,

Somehow the good Lord gives us

the power to understand

That He who holds tomorrow is

the One who holds our hand.

When your heart is heavy and your day

is full with care,

Instead of trying to escape, why not

withdraw in prayer?

For in prayer there is renewal of the

spirit, mind, and heart,

For everything is lifted up in which God

has a part.

His goodness is unfailing,

　　His kindness knows no end,

For the Lord is a good shepherd

　　on whom you can depend.

He will guard and guide and keep you

　　in His loving, watchful care,

And when traveling in dark valleys,

　　your shepherd will be there.

God grant these gifts of faith, hope, and love—

Three things this world has so little of—

For only these gifts from our Father above

Can turn our hearts from hatred to love.

When I open up my eyes

to greet another day,

I'll find myself renewed in strength

and there will open up a way

To meet what seemed impossible

for me to solve alone,

And once again I'll be assured

I am never on my own.

Deliverance from Trials

*You are my hiding place; you will
protect me from trouble and surround
me with songs of deliverance.*

PSALM 32:7

As children we were eager to take steps
out into the world; but as soon as we met
the unexpected, we ran right back to our
parents. They were the safe place where
we could hide from those things that
frightened us. God promises that we can
run to Him at any age. When your trials
and tribulations overwhelm you, look to
Him for deliverance. Make Him your safe
place. He will surround you with peace.

WHEN LIFE SEEMS EMPTY

AND THERE'S NO PLACE TO GO,

WHEN YOUR HEART IS TROUBLED

AND YOUR SPIRITS ARE LOW,

THE BURDEN THAT SEEMS TOO HEAVY TO BEAR

GOD LIFTS AWAY ON THE WINGS OF PRAYER.

For God in His goodness has promised

that the cross that He gives us to wear

Will never exceed our endurance

or be more than our strength can bear.

SECURE IN A BLESSED ASSURANCE

WE CAN SMILE AS WE FACE TOMORROW,

FOR GOD HOLDS THE KEY TO THE FUTURE,

AND NO SORROW OR CARE WE NEED BORROW.

What more can we ask of the Savior

Than to know we are never alone—

That His mercy and love are unfailing

And He makes all our problems His own.

*"And surely I am with you always,
to the very end of the age."*

MATTHEW 28:20

Sometimes the road of life seems long
 as we travel through the years
And with a heart that's broken
 and eyes brimful of tears,
We falter in our weariness
 and sink beside the way.
But God leans down and whispers,
 "Child, there'll be another day."
And the road will grow much smoother
 and much easier to face,
So do not be disheartened—
 this is just a resting place.

Wish not for the easy way
      to win your heart's desire,
For the joy's in overcoming and
      withstanding flood and fire—
For to triumph over trouble and
      grow stronger with defeat
Is to win the kind of victory
      that will make your life complete.

When the fires of life

burn deep in your heart

And the winds of destruction

seem to tear you apart,

Remember God loves you

and wants to protect you.

So seek that small haven

and be guided by prayer

To that place of protection

within God's loving care.

He will not let me go alone

Into the valley that's unknown.

Kings and kingdoms all pass away—

Nothing on earth endures.

But the love of God who sent His Son

Is forever and ever yours.

God, be my resting place
        and my protection
In hours of trouble, defeat,
        and dejection—
May I never give way
        to self-pity and sorrow,
May I always be sure
        of a better tomorrow,
May I stand undaunted, come what may,
Secure in the knowledge
        I have only to pray
And ask my Creator and Father above
To keep me serene in His grace
        and His love.

Teach us that it takes the showers
    to make the flowers grow,
And only in the storms of life
    when the winds of trouble blow
Can man, too, reach maturity
    and grow in faith and grace
And gain the strength and courage
    to enable him to face
Sunny days as well as rain,
    high peaks as well as low,
Knowing that the April showers
    will make the May flowers grow. . .
And then at last may we accept
    the sunshine and the shower,
Confident it takes them both
    to make salvation ours.

When you're troubled and worried
    and sick at heart
And your plans are upset
    and your world falls apart,
Remember God's ready
    and waiting to share
The burden you find too heavy to bear.
So with faith, let go
    and let God lead the way
Into a brighter and less troubled day.

There are times when life overwhelms us

and our trials seem too many to bear—

It is then we should stop to remember

God is standing by, ready to share

The uncertain hours that confront us

and fill us with fear and despair.

My blessings are so many,

My troubles are so few,

How can I feel discouraged

When I know that I have You?

And I have the sweet assurance

That I'll never stand alone

If I but keep remembering

I am Yours and Yours alone.

I am often weak and weary,

    and life is dark and bleak and dreary. . .

But somehow when I realize

    that He who made the sea and skies

And holds the whole world in His hand

    has my small soul in His command,

It gives me strength to try once more

    to somehow reach the heavenly door

Where I will live forevermore

    with friends and loved ones I adore.

Fulfillment

A cheerful heart is good medicine, but a crushed spirit dries up the bones.

PROVERBS 17:22

God has a plan for you, dear friend. His plan includes hope, faith, courage, blessing, and much more. He is determined to fulfill His plan in your life. Ask Him to open your eyes to all He has provided for you, to show you the purpose for which you were created. Fulfillment doesn't come from scholarly degrees, human success, financial prosperity, or any other earthly accomplishment. It comes from knowing and doing the will of God.

For as the flowering branches

depend upon the tree

To nourish and fulfill them

till they reach futurity,

We, too, must be dependent

on our Father up above,

For we are but the branches

and He's the tree of love.

WHEN WE "GIVE OURSELVES AWAY" IN

SACRIFICE AND LOVE,

WE ARE LAYING UP RICH TREASURES IN

GOD'S KINGDOM UP ABOVE.

*Carry each other's burdens, and in this
way you will fulfill the law of Christ.*

GALATIANS 6:2

ANY SACRIFICE ON EARTH

MADE IN THE DEAR LORD'S NAME,

ASSURES THE GIVER OF A PLACE IN

HEAVEN'S HALL OF FAME.

In prayer there is renewal of

the spirit, mind, and heart

For everything is lifted up

in which God has a part. . .

For when we go to God in prayer

our thoughts are rearranged,

So even though our problems have not

been solved or changed,

Somehow the good Lord gives us

the power to understand

That He who holds tomorrow is

the One who holds our hand.

Each day there are showers of blessings

Sent from the Father above,

For God is a great, lavish giver,

And there is no end to His love.

$\mathcal{N}$o matter how big

man's dreams are,

God's blessings are infinitely more,

For always God's giving is greater

Than what man is asking for.

Kneel in prayer in His presence

And you'll find no need to speak,

For softly in silent communion

God grants you the peace that you seek.

FATHER, MAKE US KIND AND WISE

SO WE MAY ALWAYS RECOGNIZE

THE BLESSINGS THAT ARE OURS TO TAKE,

THE FRIENDSHIPS THAT ARE OURS TO MAKE.

Withdrawal means renewal if we

withdraw to pray

And listen in the quietness

to hear what God will say.

Come near to God and he
will come near to you.

JAMES 4:8

If we put our problems in God's hand,

There is nothing we need understand. . .

It is enough to just believe

That what we need we will receive.

*D*ear God, You are a part of me—

You're all I do and all I see,

You're what I say and what I do,

For all my life belongs to You.

GOOD HEALTH, GOOD HUMOR,

AND GOOD SENSE,

NO ONE IS POOR

WITH THIS DEFENSE.

Each day at dawning I lift my heart high

And raise up my eyes to the infinite sky,

I watch the night vanish as a new day is born,

And I hear the birds sing

    on the wings of the morn;

I see the dew glisten in crystal-like splendor

While God, with a touch

    that is gentle and tender,

Wraps up the night and softly tucks it away

And hangs out the sun to herald a new day.

America's beloved inspirational poet laureate, **Helen Steiner Rice**, has encouraged millions of people through her beautiful and uplifting verse. Born in Lorain, Ohio, in 1900, Helen was the daughter of a railroad man and an accomplished seamstress and began writing poetry at a young age.

In 1918, Helen began working for a public utilities company and eventually became one of the first female advertising managers and public speakers in the country. In January 1929, she married a wealthy banker named Franklin Rice, who later sank into depression during the Great Depression and eventually committed suicide. Helen later said that her suffering made her sensitive to the pain of others. Her sadness helped her to write some of her most uplifting verses.

Her work for a Cincinnati, Ohio, greeting card company eventually led to her nationwide popularity as a poet when her Christmas card poem "The Priceless Gift of Christmas," was first read on the Lawrence Welk Show. Soon Helen had produced several books of her poetry that were a source of inspiration to millions of readers.

Helen died in 1981, leaving a foundation in her name to offer assistance to the needy and the elderly. Now more than twenty-five years after her death, Helen's words still speak powerfully to the hearts of readers about love and comfort, faith and hope, peace and joy.